COMPOSER
SHOWCASE
HAL LEONARD
STUDENT PIANO LIBRARY

EARLY INTERMEDIATE – LATE INTERMEDIATE LEVEL

The Best of CAROL KLOSE

FIFTEEN ORIGINAL PIANO SOLOS

BY CAROL KLOSE

ISBN 978-1-4950-2257-9

HAL•LEONARD®
CORPORATION
7777 W. BLUEMOUND RD. P.O. BOX 13819 MILWAUKEE, WI 53213

In Australia Contact:
Hal Leonard Australia Pty. Ltd.
4 Lentara Court
Cheltenham, Victoria, 3192 Australia
Email: ausadmin@halleonard.com.au

Visit Hal Leonard Online at
www.halleonard.com

T0056128

Ancient Towers

for Alex

By Carol Klose

Slowly, with majestic mystery (♩ = 69)

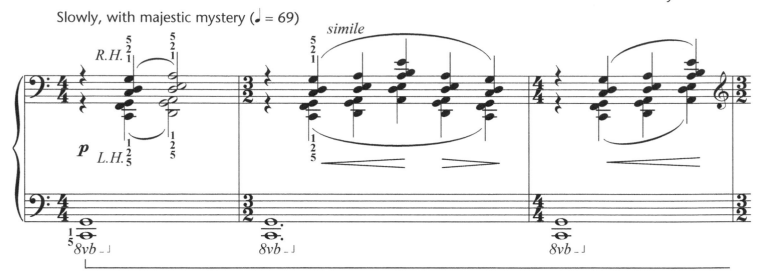

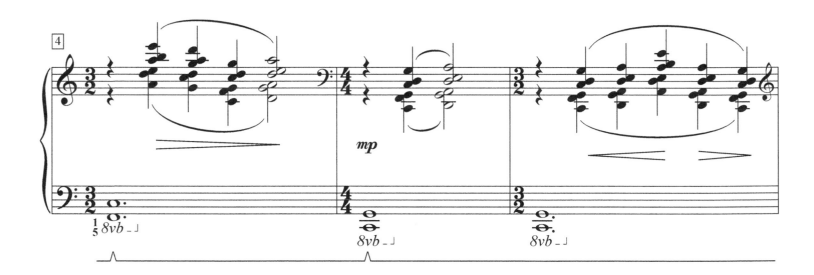

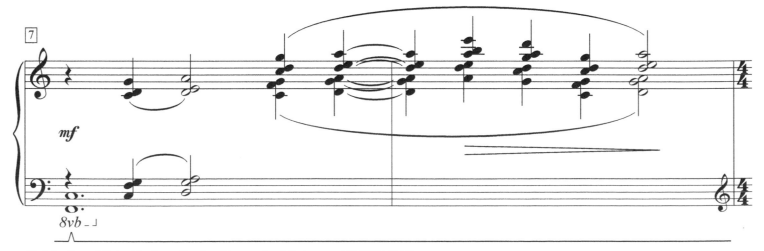

(Originally published in the collection *Watercolor Miniatures*, HL00296848)

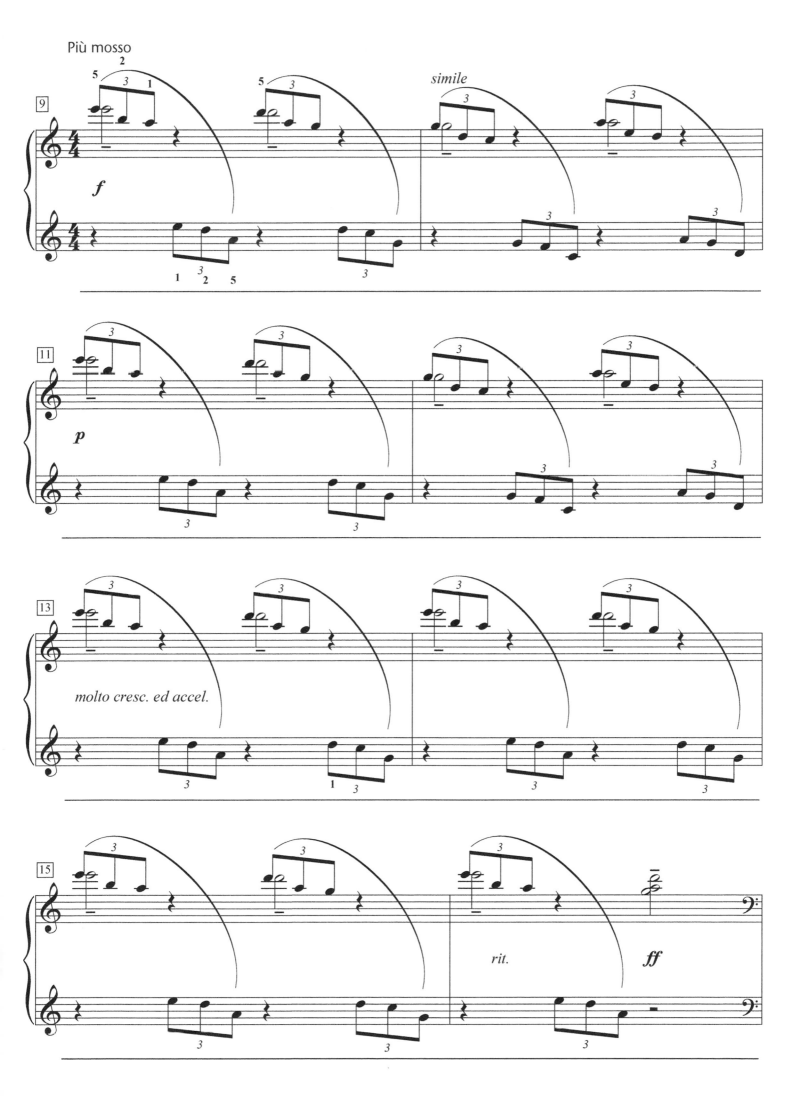

3

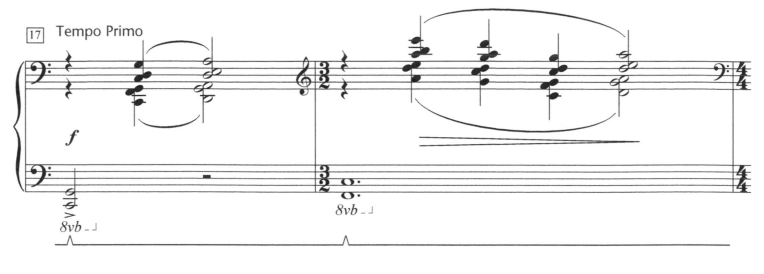

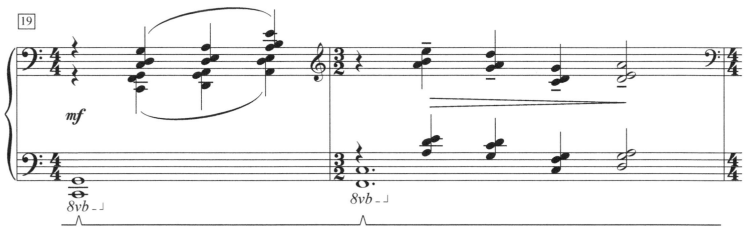

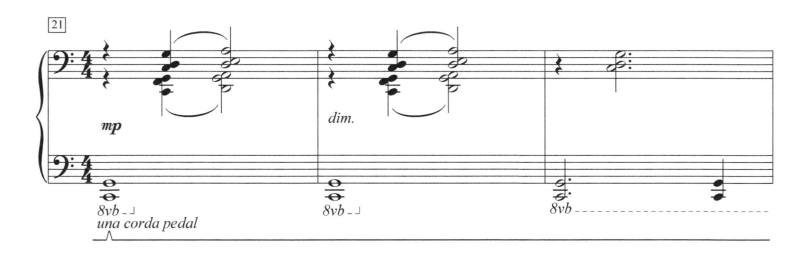

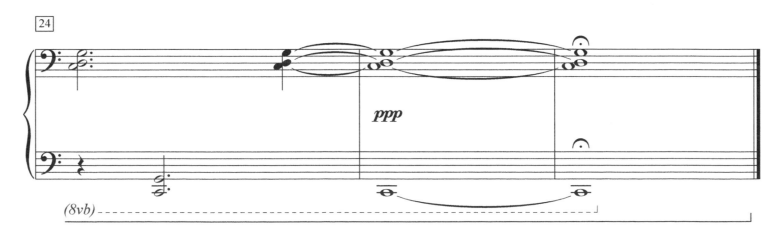

Candlelight Prelude

for my mother, Anne Jachec

By Carol Klose

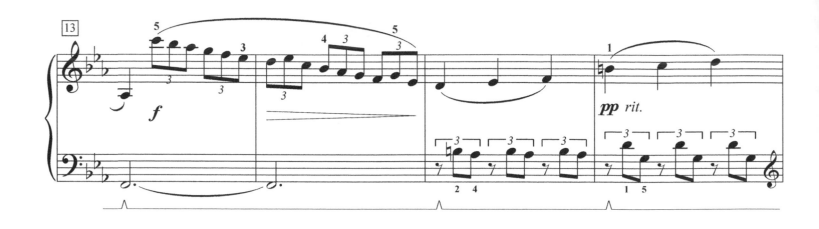

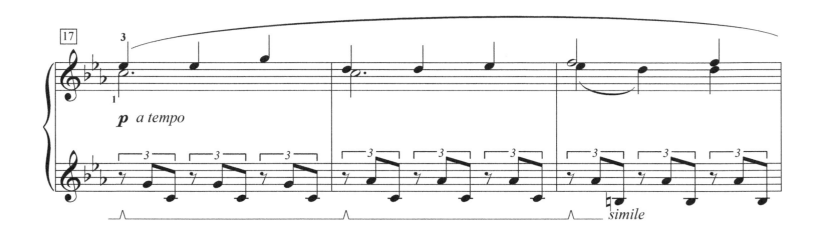

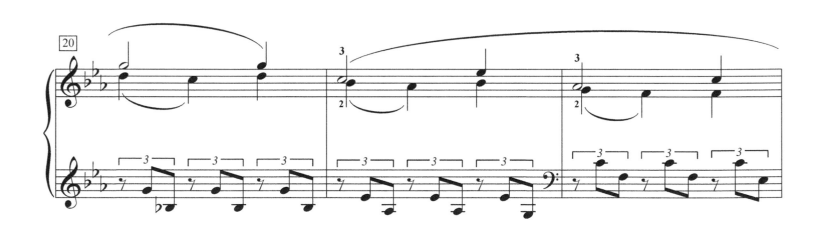

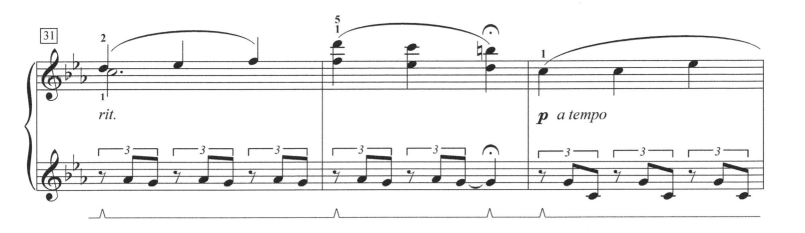

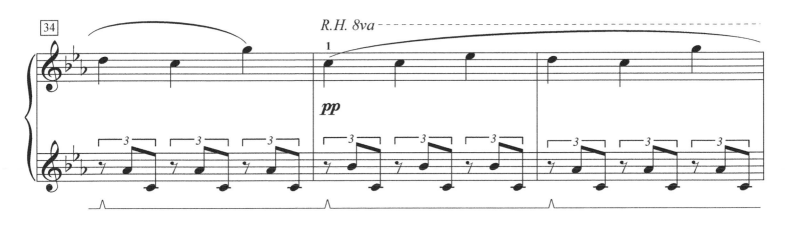

Castilian Dreamer

By Carol Klose

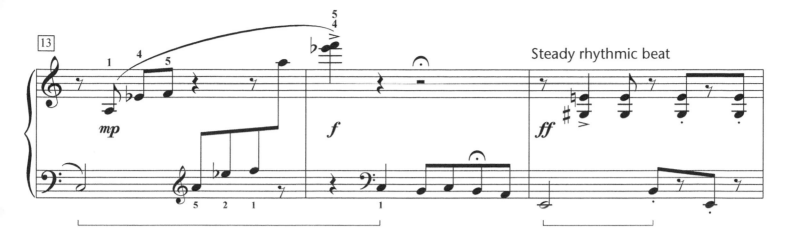

Steady rhythmic beat

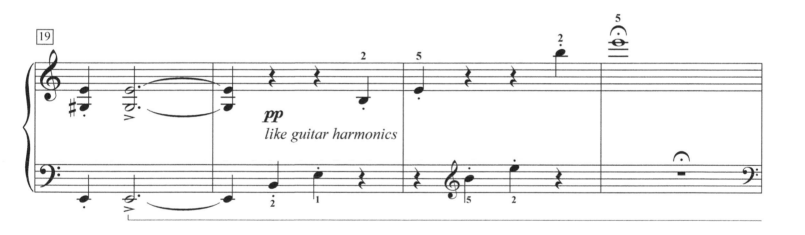

pp
like guitar harmonics

Slightly slower than beginning tempo (♩ = 72)

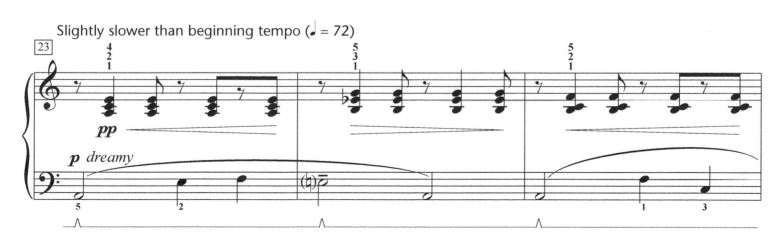

pp

p dreamy

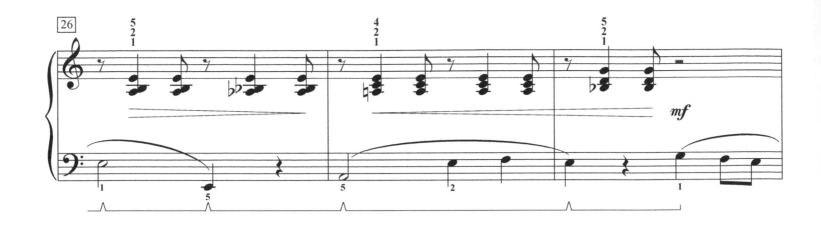

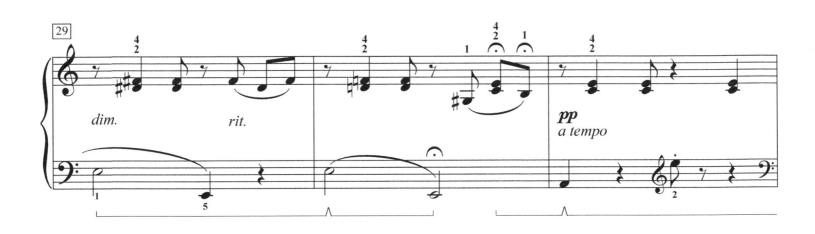

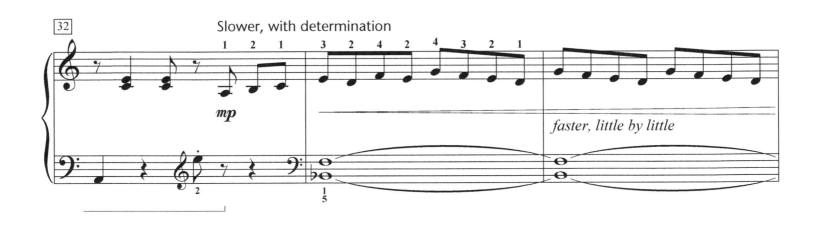

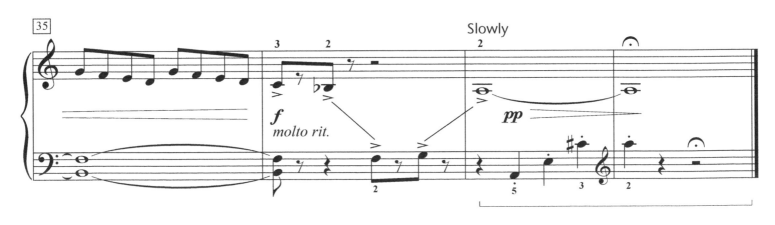

Gathering Storm Clouds

for Jane

By Carol Klose

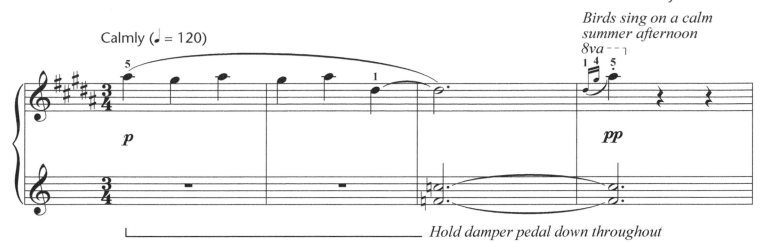

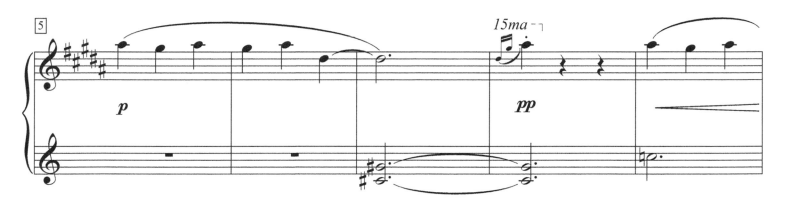

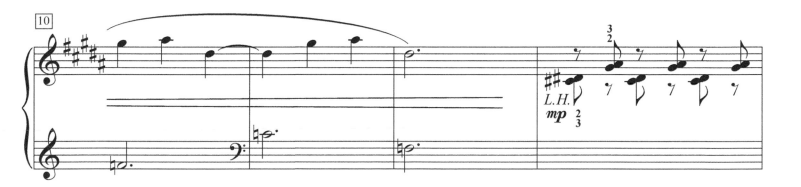

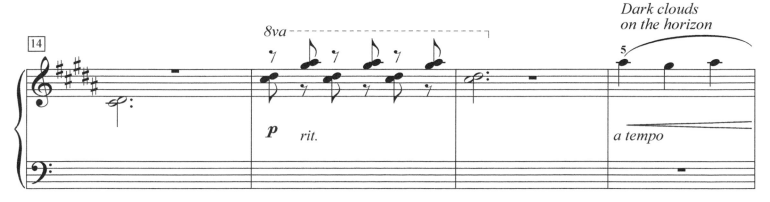

(Originally published in the collection *Watercolor Miniatures*, HL00296848)

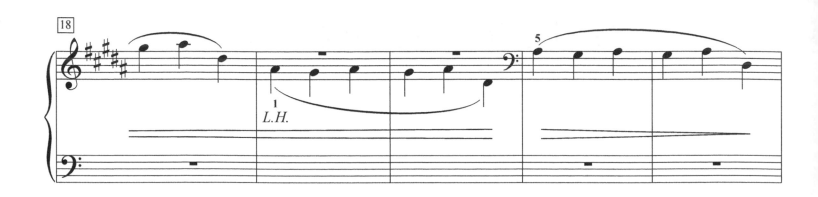

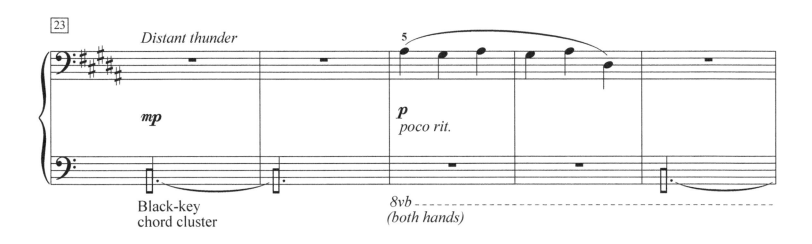

Distant thunder

mp

p
poco rit.

Black-key
chord cluster

8vb -
(both hands)

Fast and agitated, in "one" (♩ = 168)
Wind and rain begin

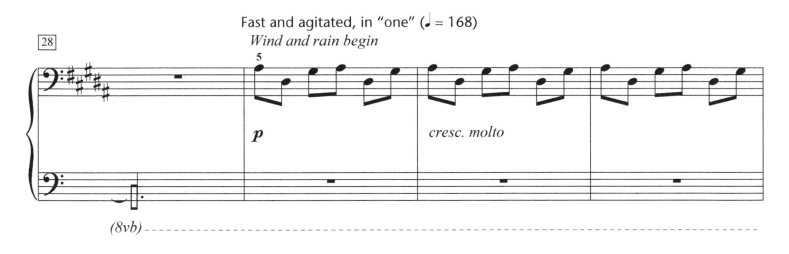

p

cresc. molto

(8vb) -

f

(8vb) -

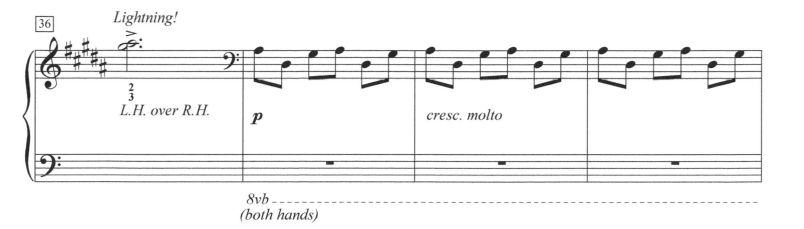

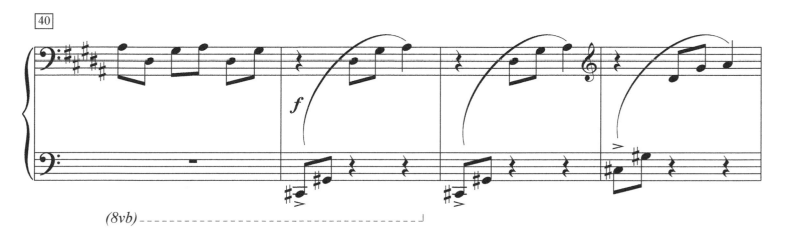

Meno mosso (♩ = 138)
The storm begins to move away

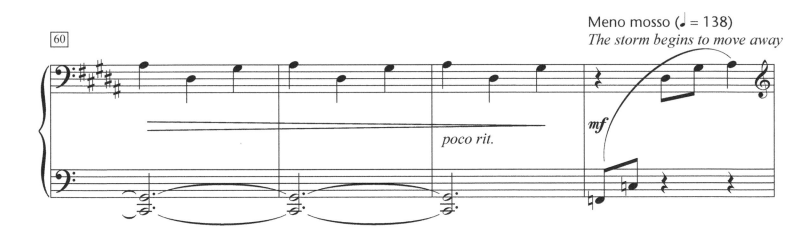

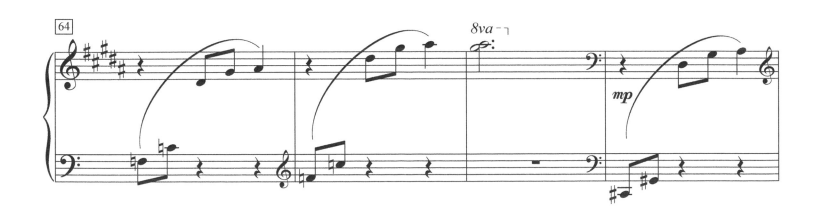

Gecko Games

Carol Klose

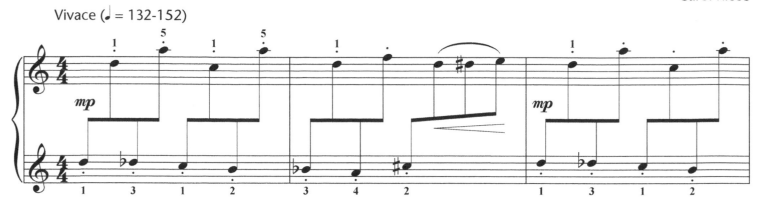

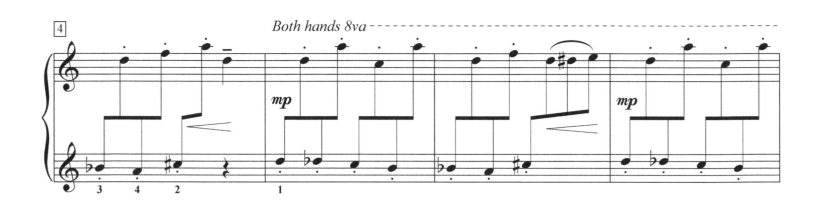

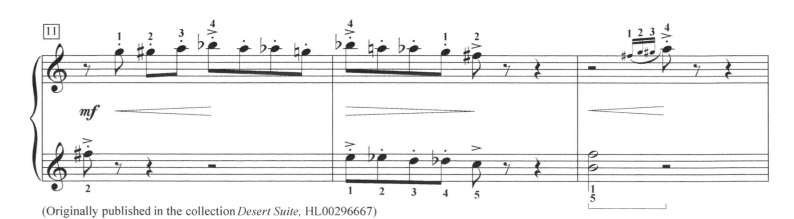

(Originally published in the collection *Desert Suite*, HL00296667)

17

Gypsy Fire

By Carol Klose

(Originally published in the collection *Romantic Expressions*, HL00296923)

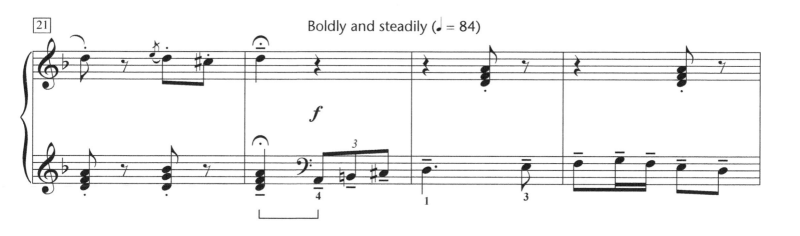

20

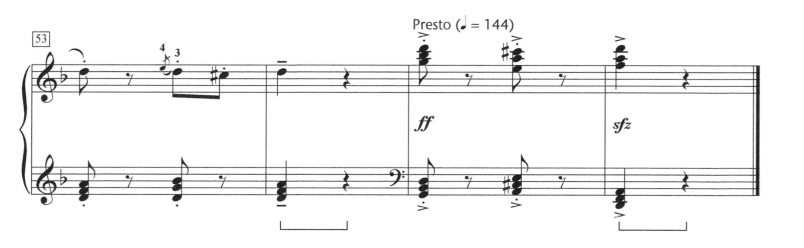

The Healing Garden

By Carol Klose

Reverently (♩ = 76-84)

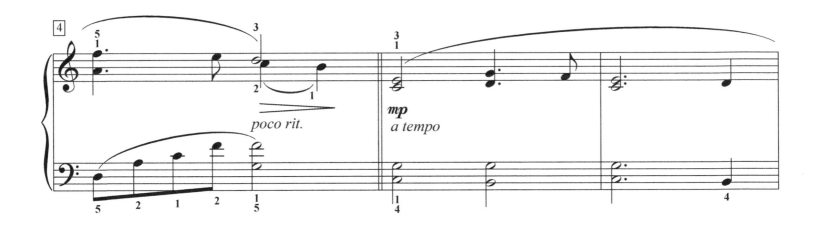

(Originally published in the collection *Garden Treasures*, HL00296787)

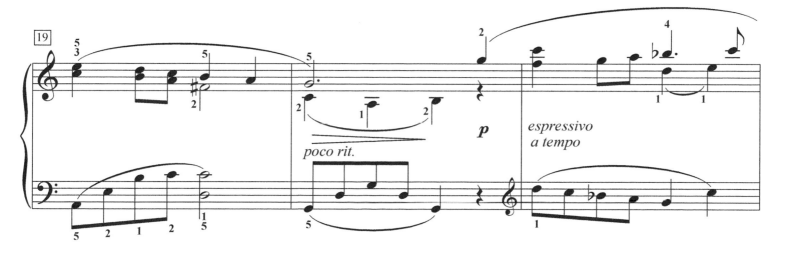

Maestro, There's a Fly in My Waltz

Carol Klose

(Originally published in the collection *Fanciful Waltzes,* HL00296473)

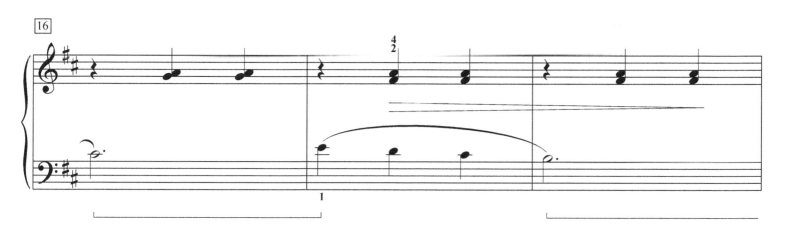

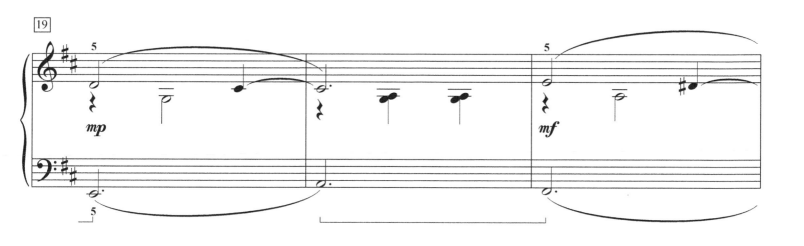

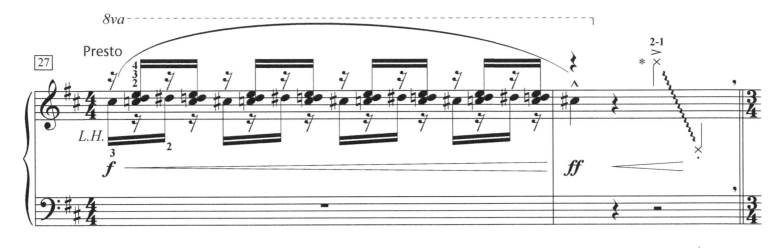

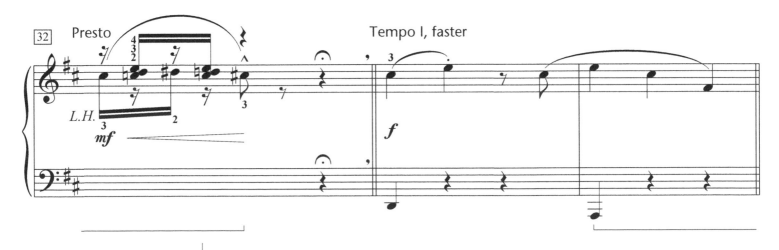

*Glissando for one beat. ✕ = approximate pitch.

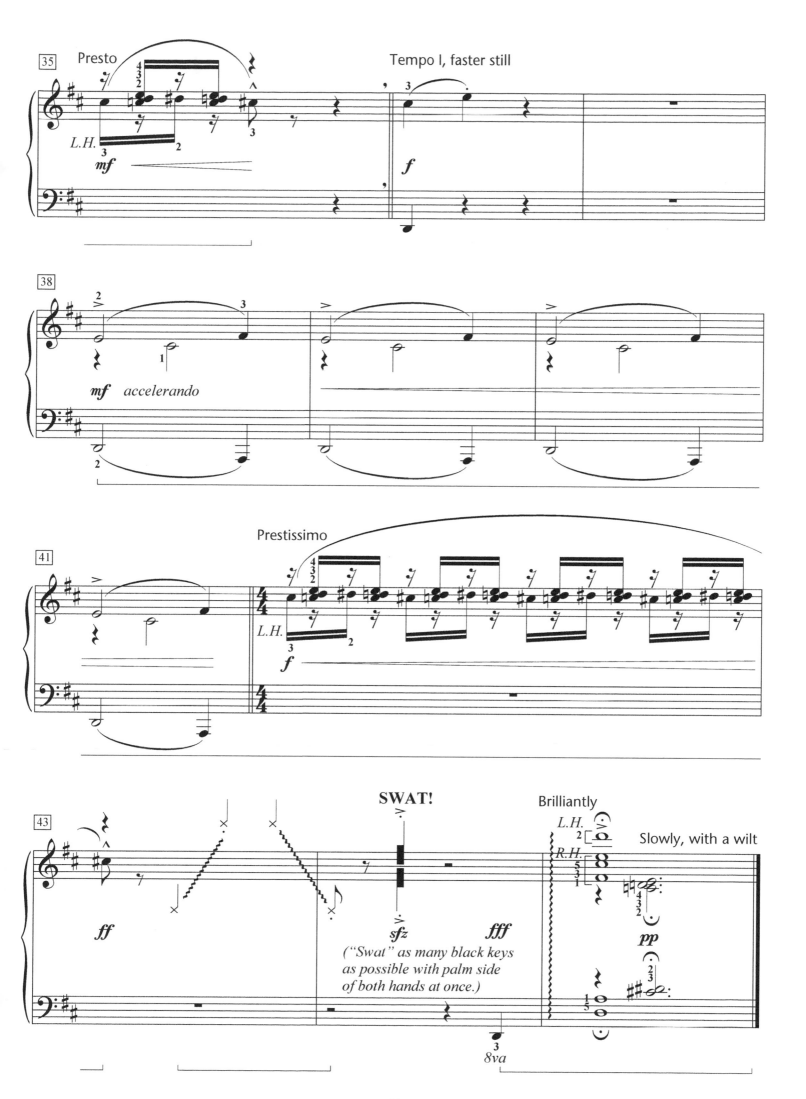

SWAT!

("Swat" as many black keys
as possible with palm side
of both hands at once.)

Mother Earth, Sister Moon

Carol Klose

(Originally published in the collection *Desert Suite*, HL00296667)

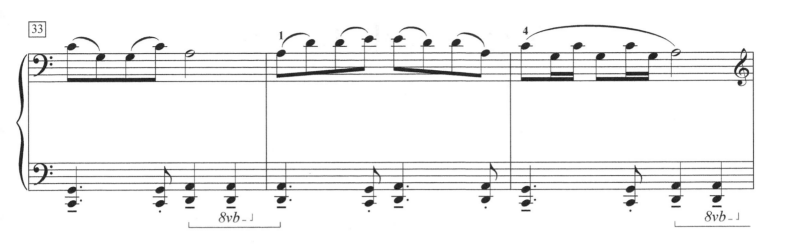

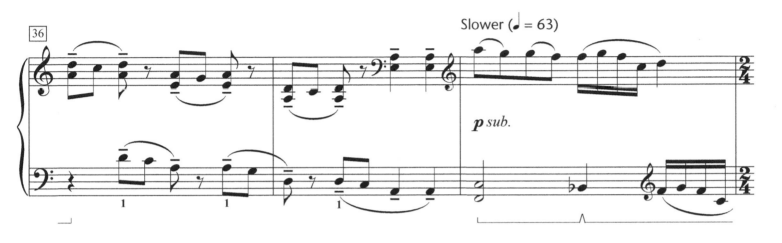

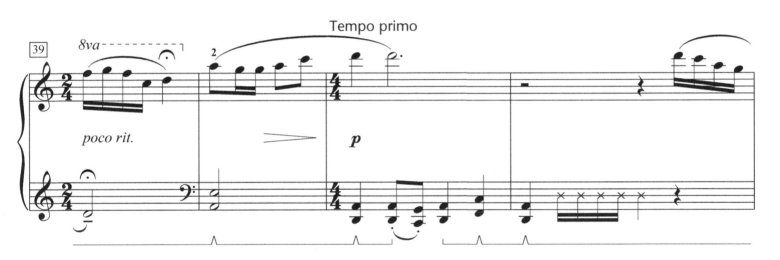

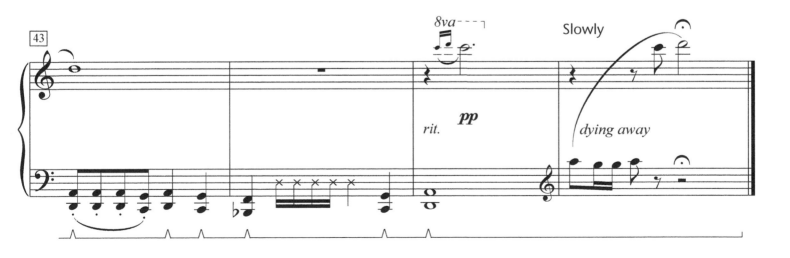

Northwoods Toccata

By Carol Klose

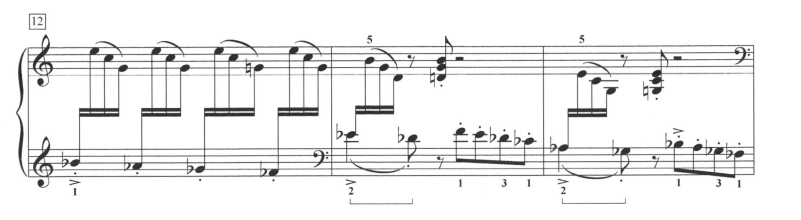

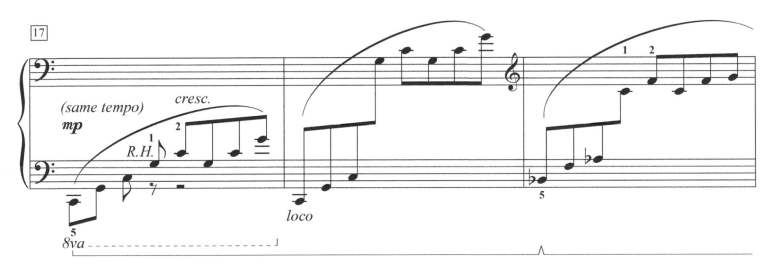

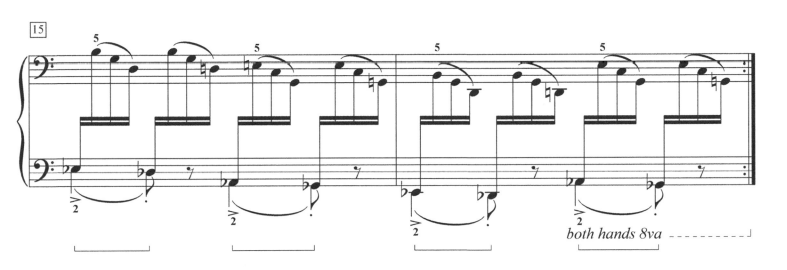

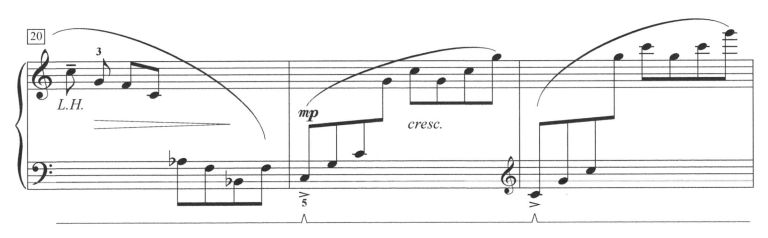

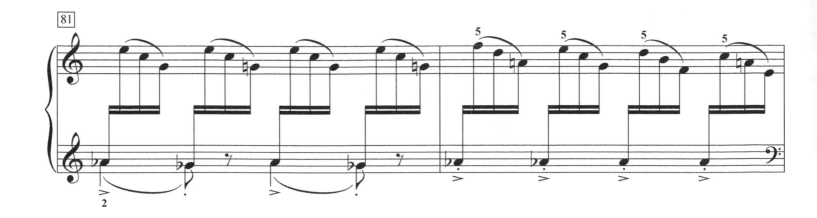

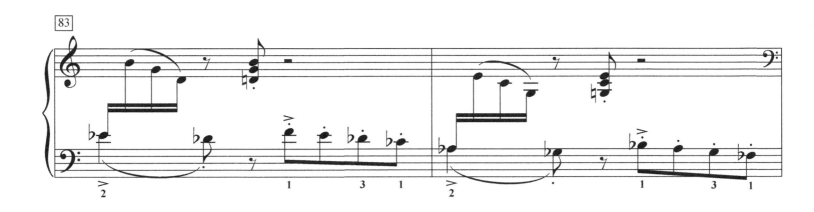

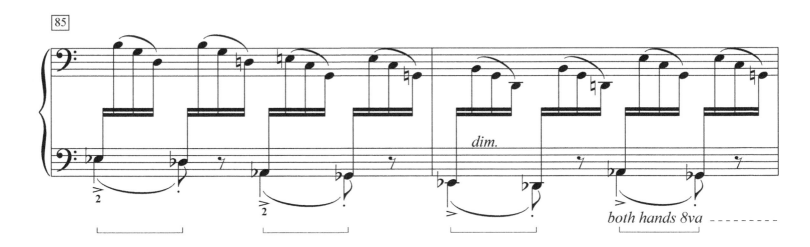

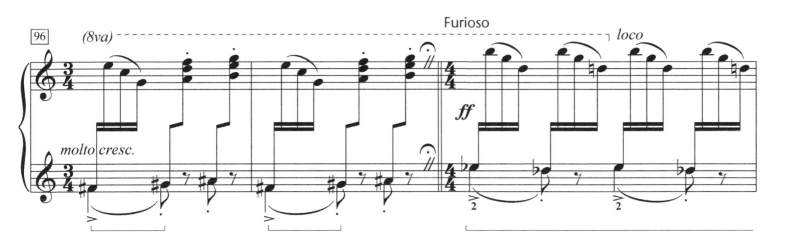

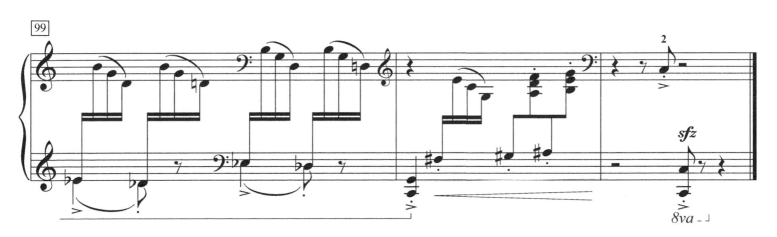

41

Prelude No. 1

Carol Klose

(Originally published in the collection *Piano Recital Showcase: Romantic Inspirations*, HL00296813)

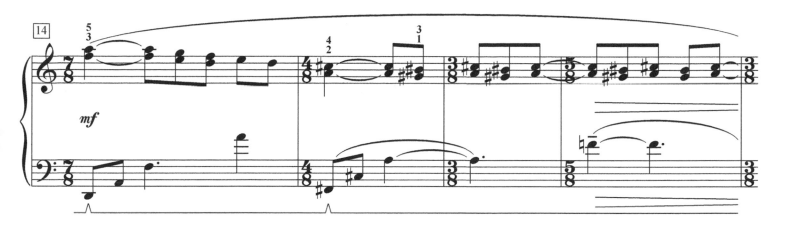

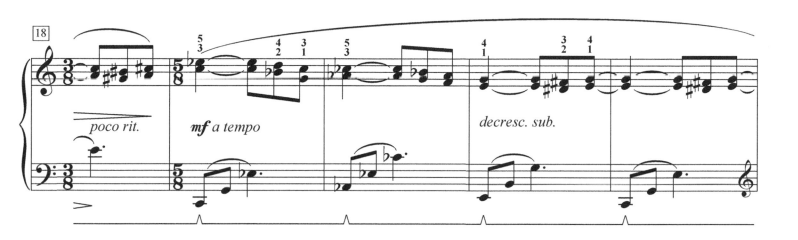

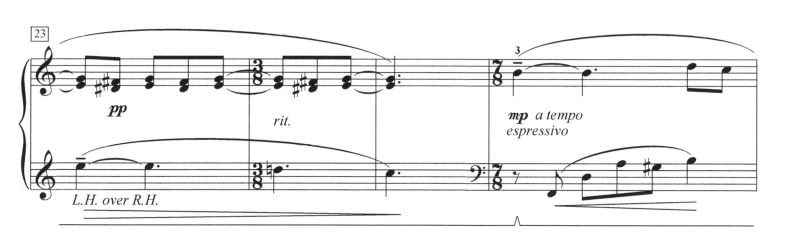

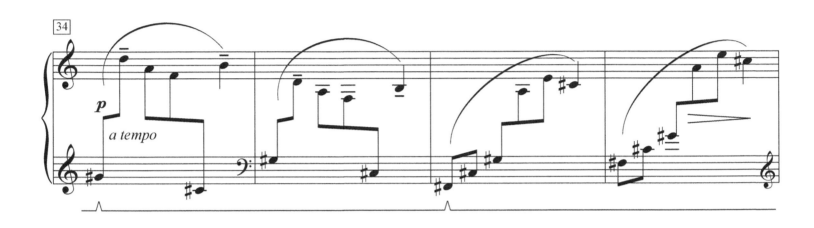

Poco più mosso

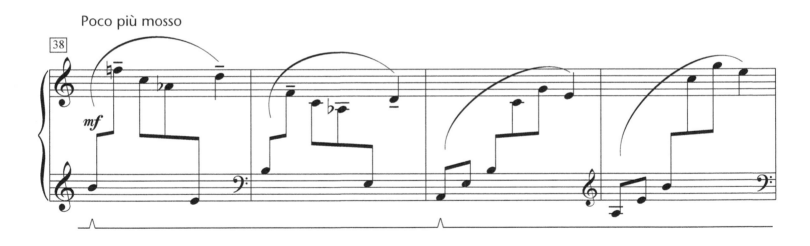

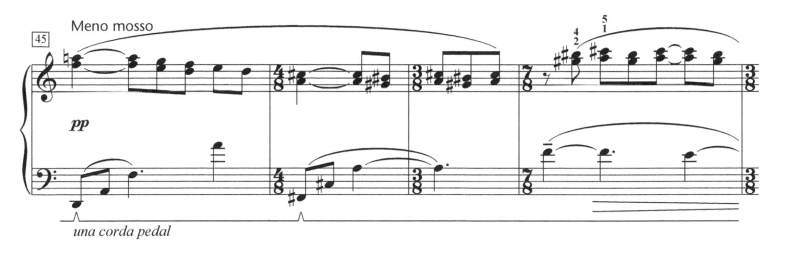

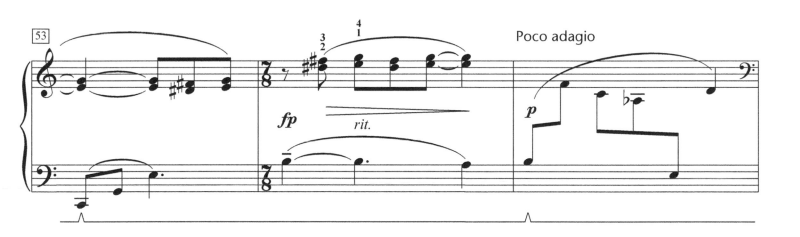

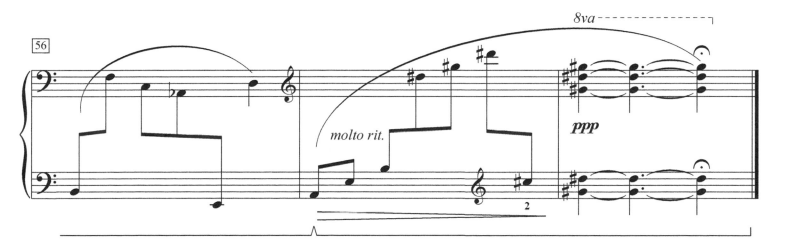

Salsa Picante

By Carol Klose

Allegro ritmico (♩ = 160-176)

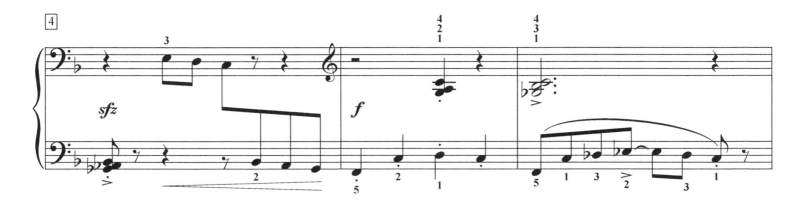

Jasmine in the Mist

for my husband John

By Carol Klose

(Originally published in the collection *Garden Treasures*, HL00296787)

Poco più mosso ($\quarternote$ =126-132)

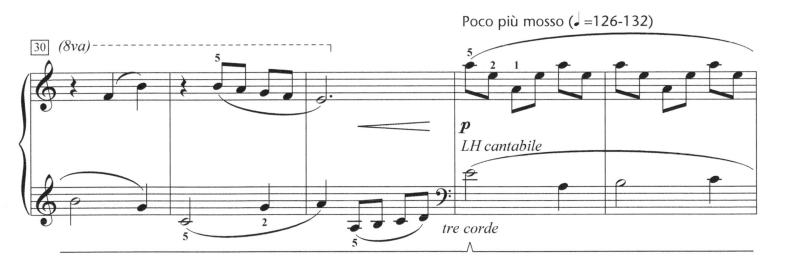

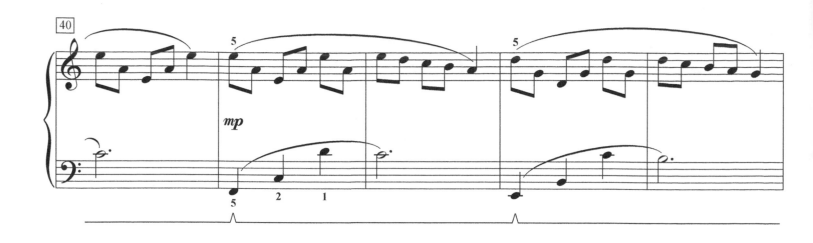

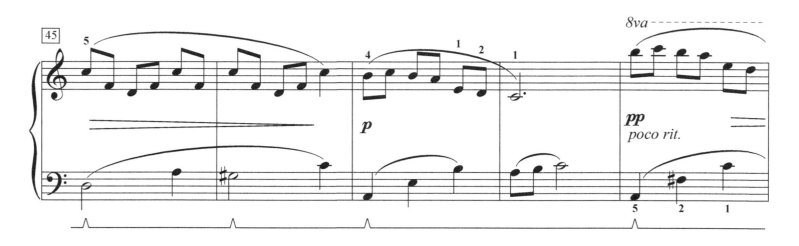

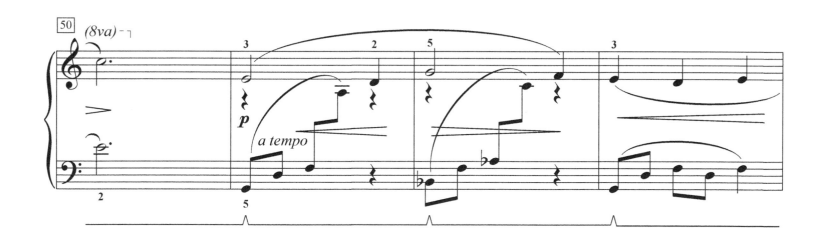

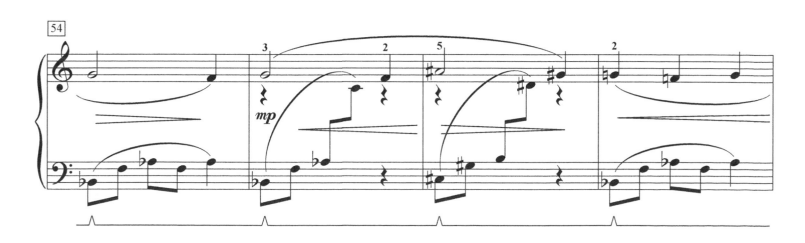

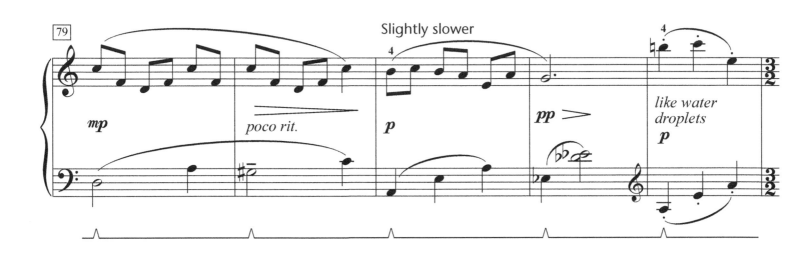

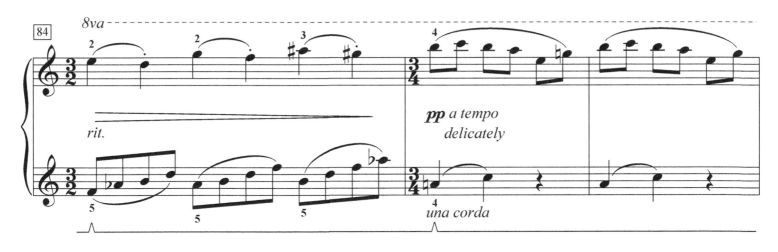

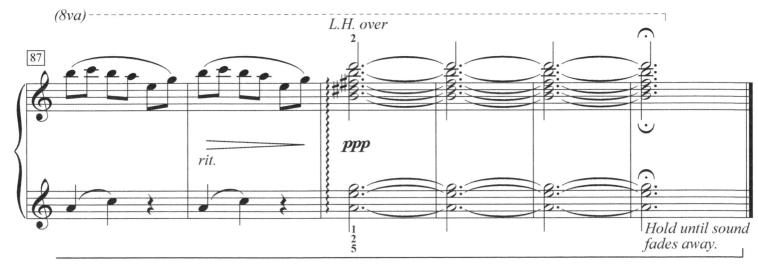

A River's Tale

Commissioned by the Piano Studio of Linda Kennedy, Maumelle, Arkansas

By Carol Klose

(Originally published in the collection *Romantic Expressions*, HL00296923)

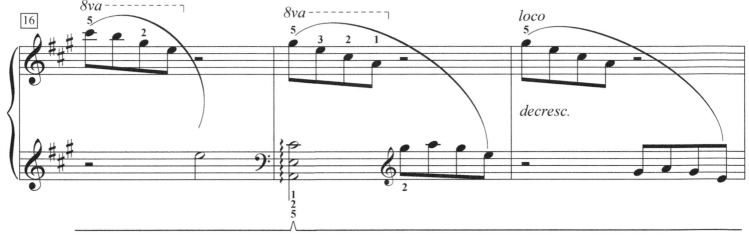

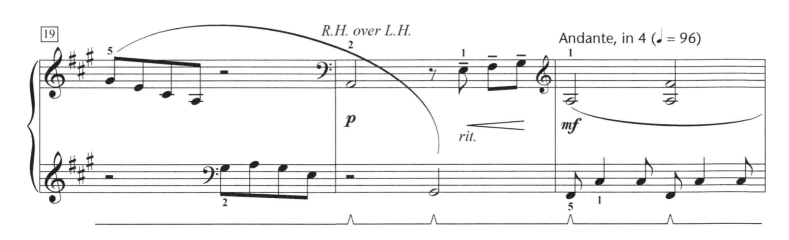

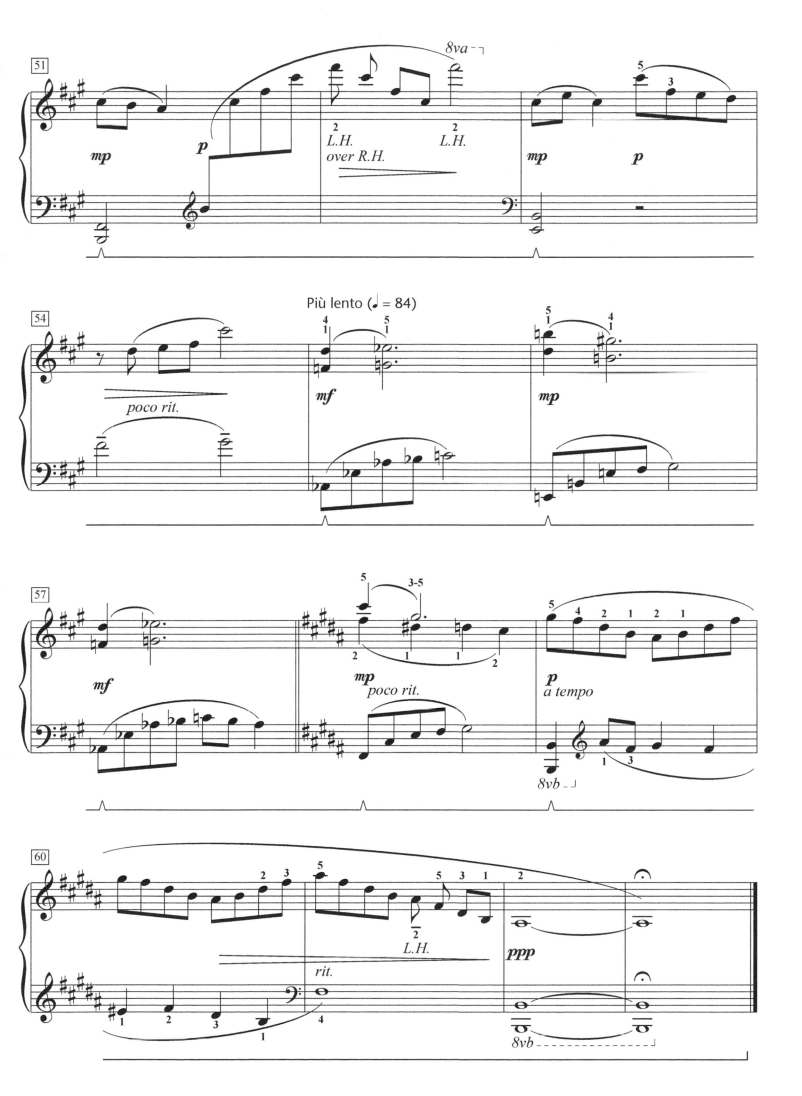

Rondo Capriccioso

Carol Klose

(Originally published in the collection *Piano Recital Showcase: Romantic Inspirations*, HL00296813)